Amazon Adventure

by Layne deMarin

Consultant:
Adria F. Klein, PhD
California State University, San Bernardino

CAPSTONE PRESS
a capstone imprint

Wonder Readers are published by Capstone Press,
1710 Roe Crest Drive, North Mankato, Minnesota 56003.
www.capstonepub.com

Books published by Capstone Press are manufactured with paper containing at least 10 percent post-consumer waste.

Library of Congress Cataloging-in-Publication Data
DeMarin, Layne.
 Amazon adventure / Layne DeMarin. — 1st ed.
  p. cm. — (Wonder readers)
 Includes index.
 ISBN 978-1-4296-7907-7 (paperback)
 ISBN 978-1-4296-8634-1 (library binding)
 1. Ecology—Amazon River Region—Juvenile literature. 2. Rain forest ecology—Amazon River Region—Juvenile literature. 3. Rain forest animals—Amazon River Region—Juvenile literature. I. Title.
 QH112.D46 2012
 577.340985'44—dc23   2011021995

Summary: Simple text and color photos introduce readers to basic information about the Amazon rain forest, its plants and animals, and how humans use its resources.

Note to Parents and Teachers

The Wonder Readers: Science series supports national science standards. These titles use text structures that support early readers, specifically with a close photo/text match and glossary. Each book is perfectly leveled to support the reader at the right reading level, and the topics are of high interest. Early readers will gain success when they are presented with a book that is of interest to them and is written at the appropriate level.

Printed in the United States of America in North Mankato, Minnesota.
102011   006405CGS12

Table of Contents

What Is a Rain Forest?

Welcome to the **rain forest**. It rains all year here. Most rain forests are near the **equator**. It is very wet and warm here.

This is the **Amazon River**. It is in the Amazon rain forest in South America. The Amazon rain forest is the biggest rain forest in the world.

Plants of the Rain Forest

Plants grow everywhere in a rain forest. Plants love the warm, wet **climate**. That is where they grow best.

All of these plants make shade.
It can be very dark in some parts
of a rain forest. Plants that
grow in the shade can live
without much sunlight.

Trees are the tallest plants
in a rain forest. Some rain forest
trees can grow to be more than
100 feet (30 meters) tall.

Other rain forest plants grow in the trees. Flowers called **orchids** grow on tree branches. Orchids come in many colors and sizes.

Lianas are vines that wrap around the trees. The vines climb up the tree trunks to get to the sunlight.

orchids   **lianas**

Animals of the Rain Forest

Many animals live in the rain forest.
Some are small. Some are big.
Some live down low. Some live up high.
This capybara lives on the ground.

These animals live in the trees.
A scarlet macaw is a bird
with brightly colored feathers.
A tree boa is almost the same color
as the leaves on the trees.

 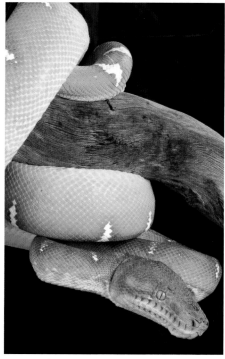

scarlet macaw **emerald tree boa**

Sloths also live in the trees.
They eat leaves. They slowly climb
the branches to reach their food.

Monkeys are also good climbers.
This noisy monkey makes
howling sounds. It is called
a howler monkey.

People of the Rain Forest

People live in the rain forest too.
They build their houses
using trees and other plants.

They make boats and travel
the rivers in them. It is hard
to build roads through
all the rain forest plants.

The tall trees that grow in the rain forest are good for building. Some people worry that cutting down trees is not good. Trees are important to the rain forest **ecosystem**.

A rain forest is a very special kind of ecosystem. It makes our world a beautiful and healthy place to live.

Glossary

Amazon River   river in South America; one of the largest in the world

climate   the usual weather of a place

ecosystem   all the plants and animals that make up an area

equator   an imaginary line that goes around the middle of Earth

liana   a type of vine

orchid   a type of flower

rain forest   a thick forest where it rains all year long

Now Try This!

Imagine what it would be like to go on your own adventure in the Amazon. Get a blank note card to use as a postcard. Draw something you might see on your adventure on one side of the card. Write a letter to someone back home describing your trip on the back of the card.

Internet Sites

FactHound offers a safe, fun way to find Internet sites related to this book. All of the sites on FactHound have been researched by our staff.

Here's all you do:

Visit *www.facthound.com*

Type in this code: 9781429686341

Super-cool stuff! Check out projects, games and lots more at
www.capstonekids.com

Index

Editorial Credits

Maryellen Gregoire, project director; Mary Lindeen, consulting editor; Gene Bentdahl, designer; Sarah Schuette, editor; Wanda Winch, media researcher; Eric Manske, production specialist

Photo Credits

Dreamstime: Paura, 14; iStockphoto Inc: Abinormal, 7, Atelopus, 6, HHakim, 1; Shutterstock: Audrey Snider-Bell, 11 (right), Carlos Neto, 15, Dr. Morley Read, 4, 8, 9 (right), E. Sweet, 10, ecoventurestravel, 16, Eugene Berman, cover, jaana piira, 13, Johnny Lye, 5, Mariusz S. Jurgielewicz, 17, slowfish, 9 (left), worldswildlifewonders, 11 (left), 12

Word Count: **346**   Guided Reading Level: **K**   Early Intervention Level: **19**